Come and S[ail] with Me

Written by Lisa Thompson
Pictures by Craig Smith

Come and sail with me.

One gold coin for your barrel.

Come and sail with me.

Two gold coins for your barrel.

Come and sail with me.

Three gold coins for your barrel.

Come and sail with me.

Four gold coins for your barrel.

Come and sail with me.

Five gold coins for your barrel.

Come and sail with me.

Six gold coins for your barrel.

Come and sail with me.

No gold coins for your barrel!